Masonic Meditations
Vol. 3

The Work

Edited and Compiled by

RaMen

Authored by Dr. Jeff Menzise, 32°

Masonic Meditations Vol 3 - The Work

10 9 8 7 6 5 4 3 2 1

Cover Artwork & Design by Jeffery Menzise, Ph.D. for Mind on the Matter Publishing

Library of Congress Cataloging-in-Publication Data
Menzise, Jeffery,
        Masonic Meditations Vol 3 - The Work/ by Jeff Menzise, Ph.D.
includes Foreword, Cover Artwork, & Design

ISBN: 978-0-9856657-9-1

Published in 2019 by
Mind on the Matter Publishing,
PO BOX 755, College Park, MD 20741
Website: www.mindonthematter.com
Email: drjeff@mindonthematter.com
Instagram & Twitter: @drjeffmenzise
Office Phone: 240-988-9639

Dedication

This book is dedicated to those truth seekers who journey through life seeking the answers to the questions that puzzle us all. I hope this series provides you with inspiration, insight, a thought-provoking exchange, and perhaps, answers.

Acknowledgment

We would like to thank the Phylaxis Society, the Phylaxis Magazine, Lux e Tenebris, as well as the Masonic Digest (published out of the Most Worshipful Prince Hall Grand Lodge of the District of Columbia) for originally publishing many of the thoughts shared in this series. We would also like to thank those who have requested a collection of Masonic writings authored by Dr. Jeff Menzise. We hope this response is sufficient.

Preface

This series presents an introductory view of my thoughts as both an initiate of several African spiritual systems, and an initiate up to the 32nd degree of the Scottish Rite and 10th degree of the York Rite, Prince Hall Freemasonry. The purpose for writing and now compiling this series is simply to offer an opinion and perspective on matters related to Freemasonry. The views that I provide are original but not necessarily unique, meaning, you may find similar statements shared by other Masonic and non-Masonic philosophers, authors, and scholars. The originality is in how I express these thoughts from my unique perspective having studied various philosophical systems, including the science of clinical psychology.

This three volume series is divided into the following subjects: Symbolism, Philosophy, and The Work. As a symbolist, I often seek the deeper meaning of both form and function; this is the theme running through volume one. Because Freemasonry is largely based on the symbolic form of communication, it has served as a field rich in resources for me to interpret and translate. The main feature of volume two, on philosophy, is a deep-dive into my views on the origins of Freemasonry as a system of human development. Finally, in volume three, I explore how the science of meditation and self-reflection is beneficial to Freemasons, within the context of our Craft.

There is something for everyone in this series. The wisdom and insights offered are universal and easily adapted to any existing religious and philosophical system or orientation. The practical tools offered alongside the cognitive exercise of reading each of the articles, is enough to form a new perspective for those who choose to engage the text on a deeper level.

Contents & Articles

Operating
on
Speculations

Jeff Menzise, Ph.D., 32°, FPS

*I*n our craft, we often pride ourselves on representing the Speculative form of Freemasonry, as opposed to the Operative; that somehow the speculation has greater, more noble and glorious purposes than the operations themselves. Is the head side of a coin any more valuable than the tails? Sure, if a person is betting on one over the other. Otherwise, intrinsically speaking they are equal and both necessary for the existence of the other. As the saying goes: There is no such thing as a one-sided coin.

In regards to Speculative and Operative Freemasonry, the same is true. There would be no operative craft without the speculation that designed it. Likewise, the speculative would not exist were it incapable of being operationalized (i.e., put to action). And thus we have the ongoing love story of the complementary nature of all of creation.

Contrary to popular belief, and what we all learn as we are being i....., p....., and r......., Operative Masonry is the intentional use of our spiritual, mental and physical talents towards the manifestation or modification of our intentions. Simply stated, Operative Masonry goes beyond bricklaying and stone building; it is the actual manifestation of our mental and spiritual qualities. Imagine, if you will, the level of skill that it takes to know materials and how they interact with one another for the purpose of building. This is the architect's profession.

Now, take that same concept and apply it to spiritual and mental architecture. Recognize how our bodies naturally possess the knowledge of specific materials (in this case, vitamins, minerals, proteins, oils, etc.), using it to build our temples made "without the sound of tools." This too, is Operative Masonry, although the connection is veiled. So much has been removed from our Ancient teachings that we no longer shine as we could. Instead we agree to call rust stainless steel, and value pyrite as a treasure equal to gold.

Think back to our elders who actually built in stone, bricks, and wood. Acknowledge the nobility inherent in the souls of those Brothers; the men who know how to smooth and balance the rough ashlar and align the bricks, building fortresses, temples, and monuments to the G. A. O. T. U. The comprehensive knowledge of this truly divine gift is expressing itself both scientifically and artistically.

There is something powerful in this art, which becomes even more powerful when performed with a deeper understanding of who and what we actually are as Freemasons; specifically as descendants of the African Lodge. Scattered around the planet are shining examples of how, by combining the operative and speculative into one ritual process, civilization and its individual citizenry are elevated into their full potential of God-given talents.

In our Standard Monitor, we are told of three major orders of architecture that were discovered by the Greeks and the two additional added by the Romans. This lesson, starting with the Greeks, negates the plethora of columns and buildings (temples, monuments) that remain observable throughout the Nile Valley in North East Africa. This concrete evidence identifies an earlier and more Ancient Order of Architecture (Masonry). Much like the later Greek and Roman columns, the Kemetic (Egyptian) columns were of various types with a multitude of designs depending on their use and location.

Throughout Kemet (Egypt) you

will find columns crowned by papyrus and lotus plants. You will also find columns carved with the ancient principles known as Neteru (prime-creative energies). For example, in the Temple of Denderah, you'll find columns with the face of Het Heru [Hathor] carved at the top.

In other symbolism, you'll find a column known as the "Djed pillar," representing the strength of the erect back of a noble man. There are also large numbers of columns, literally coated with the sacred teachings of the ancient sages, etched deep into stone, beyond the reach of the profane.

The "masonic" temples lining the Nile River are monumental proof of how one could prosper by combining operative and speculative knowledge into a singular craft. These monuments are known to symbolize, on one level, the divinity found in the human being striving towards perfection of their temples (Figure 1). This is similar to how the tetragrammaton (the unspeakable Hebrew word for "God") can be written to symbolize God dwelling in man (Figure 2.)

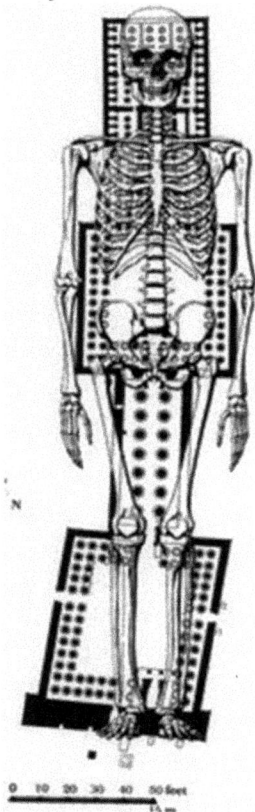

Figure 1. Temple of Luxor overlaying the human skeleton.

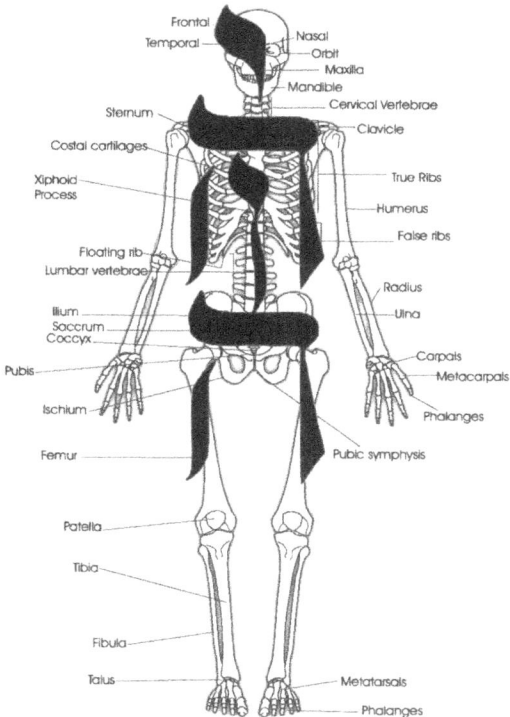

Figure 2. The tetragrammaton overlaying the human skeleton.

Kabbalistically speaking, the tetragrammaton is a formula, and each letter has both a mathematical and symbolical interpretation; we shall devote our attention to the latter. The Yod (ﬗ), which sometimes replaces the "G" in the compass and square (and is found inside the triangle on the 14th degree ring), has multiple interpretations and representations, including: all manifested power, the potential for manifestation, and even the hand of man (a main tool used for mani-festing and mani-pulating reality; "mani-" means "hand" in Latin, and is used to work upon materials). The significance of the Yod (ﬗ) being at the head is the fact that most profound works often begin in the mental realm (Speculative), and are later *mani*fested in physical forms (Operative).

Further, its duality, the manifested and potentially manifested, represents the masculine and feminine nature of all things. Lastly, the head, more specifically the pineal gland and/or the crown chakra

18

are considered to be the main entrance and exit point of the spirit/soul into and out from the body.

Next, the Hau (⎯⎯) represents the vital essence, or that which vitalizes all living things. In certain Eastern systems it is known as Chi, Qi, Prana, and Kundalini. In Ancient Egyptian it is called Ra and Ankh. This universal symbol and reality of vitality is apparent in all things alive and moving. Particle physicists have made it very plain that all things that "are," are in fact moving, based on the vibration of their molecular components. So whether a rock or a tree, a goat or a Noble, all things are blessed with this vital essence; yes, even the dying, in their decay, maintain the presence of this universal and mysterious force.

One of the main points of entry, of this vital essence into the body, is via the complementary activity of lungs and heart, that is, breathing and circulation. Of course we also get it from the foods we eat, however, I would dare say the more important route is breathing. The average person can only hold their breath for a matter of minutes before they begin to suffer irreparable damage to their brains and organs. On the other hand, people have gone for days, and even weeks without food and/or water. This example demonstrates the value of the breathed Chi as compared to the digested.

Additionally, breathing is one of the few automatic bodily processes that can be manipulated via the Will. The Hau (ה), as it relates to the symbol of Man, represents the shoulder blades, the trunk and the abdominal cavity. Interestingly enough, this is where both the heart and lungs are grown and protected.

Next is the Vau (ו), a symbol of Light, signifying the eye of man (one of the organs designed to process and inter-act with light). It is also sometimes used to symbolize the ear and the sound of air/wind. Lastly, it is sometimes used to denote the most profound of all myster-ies, those things that are not only difficult to fathom, but also those things that are unknown as options for contemplation. In the diagram above, the Vau (ן) is directly in line with the spinal column with its upper most point overlaying the location of the solar plexus. Officially known as the celiac plexus, this focal point for nerve fibers and even arterial and venous branches, is the location of one of the body's most profound energy centers. According to Traditional Chinese Medicine, it is also a gateway or portal entering into regions of the energetic body. The Vau (ן) closely resembles the Yod (י) resting atop a curved line, which could symbolize the energies being distributed from the Yod (י), through the Hau (ה), down the Vau (ן) and into the rest of the body (similar to the central nervous system).

Its importance is demonstrated by how the nervous, circulatory, and respiratory systems (via the diaphragm) are all focused into this one area. It is a focal point, gathering all of the divine representations that Man carries as an offspring of the Creator. It is via this profound region (the solar plexus), that we gather the heart, energy, and mobility to do all that is done.

This understanding leads us to the final letter, the second Hau (ה). Carrying the same attributes as the first, this second Hau (ה) begins with the pelvic region and ends with the legs. The pelvic region of the body houses and nurtures the reproductive organs, and in females, is precisely the structure that undergoes extreme anatomical and physiological changes during pregnancy and birth. The line of the Vau (ו) empties directly into the pelvis and may be distributed down either or both legs, or perhaps into the world as an entirely new manifestation (recall the meaning of the Yod [י] as discussed above).

This region, specifically the sexual organs, is thought to be the most sensitive aspect of the human body. Sensitivity is nothing more than the degree to which stimulation is necessary in order to generate excitation, awareness and arousal of the nervous and other tissues of a particular region. Similar to the vital essence of the first Hau (冂), this Hau (冂) represents the same vital essence as a function of the reproductive potential and processes.

There is an acupuncture point at the root chakra (located in the perineum) that also serves as a bandas. In Hindu meditation practices, the bandas are contracted, becoming a lock that prevents vitality from leaking out of the body. This same point, when contracted, is also used to prevent the ejaculation of semen during a male orgasm (an action that is known to drain the life force from a man... this may be why men fall asleep and crave food following an ejaculation, and why athletes are discouraged from having sex before a competition).

This key helps to recognize that God dwells in the living temple of "Man." It is one of the most profound mysteries to be pondered, as we journey as Speculative Masons learning to actualize, or render Operative, the various tools of our Craft. With the understanding that the G. A. O. T. U. (God) dwells within our very beings, and the fact that the G. A. O. T. U. fashioned such a miraculous vehicle (the body) within which to travel, it makes sense that our practically applied lessons help to maintain optimal performance.

In light of this fact, the remainder of this article will focus on taking our Craft from Speculative to Operational. We'll do this by looking closely at a few of our tools, in order to identify how our Speculative understanding of their "mundane" (Operative) use, can be transformed to the level of a "speculative operation."

The Level

Operatively, the level is used to prove horizontals and establish horizons. Our more noble and glorious use of the level is to remember that our time here on earth is both linear and limited; flowing from birth to that "undiscovered country from whose bourn no traveler returns."

This concept was illustrated by Ancient Africans who applied their operative and speculative understanding to the rising and setting of the sun. Each time the sun crossed the horizon was a significant transition and passage of time that continued infinitely, and could be used as a tool to measure one's own growth, development, and progress.

In *The Mysteries of Ra*, when Ra first crosses the eastern horizon in the morning, He is actually returning (being resurrected) from the Duat (land of souls). When He reaches His zenith, He is said to be at His prime, shining in full glory (as the JW in the S). Once He descends towards the western horizon, He is said to be returning to His source, more wise than when he was first raised. Understanding this concept, one can also incorporate our knowledge of the 24-inch gauge, a tool reminding us to use our time productively and wisely, by intentionally assigning the hours of the day to very specific goals, or more profoundly, to the stages of life (which again, are based on the rising and setting of the sun).

The Plumb

Speculatively, we are reminded to walk uprightly by the symbol of the plumb. Operatively, we see that the plumb is a device for trying perpendiculars which, although made simple by the tool, is a deep evaluation of how the rise relates to the horizontal. To combine the speculative and operative nature of this symbol, we must figure out how to apply this "deep evaluation" to our personal walk, daily.

How do we understand and master the mystery behind our behaviors and choices, and make sure that we are "flying straight"? This is done by careful observation and by a steady anchor, similar to how a surveyor uses their plumb. The lead weight, based on how it hangs, determines the angle created by the two related objects; in our speculative craft, these objects are our character and knowledge.

Before receiving Light, we were like beast walking horizontally; but once resurrected, we have the chance to balance the plumb and represent the true upright nature of our potential. As a side note, it is very interesting that the word "plumb" derives from the Latin word for the metal "lead," plumbum; this is why the symbol for lead, on the Periodic Table, is **Pb**. This is important because lead is one of the metals worked upon by alchemists and transformed, or transmuted, into the perfected metal, gold.

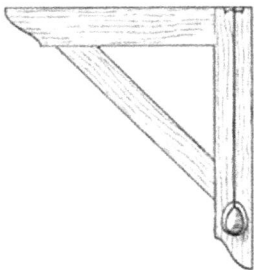

Figure 3. A Plumb Square

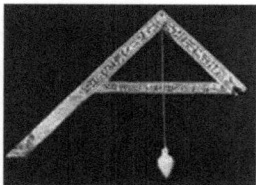

Figure 4. An Ancient Egyptian Plumb Square

<u>The Square</u>

It is no mistake that we were r.............. from the d..............to a living p...........on a s............... Every regular Mason has experienced this. As an Operative tool, the square primarily used to measure the accuracy of right angles. It is used to try surfaces in order to determine its straightness and correspondence to an adjacent surface. In our Speculative craft, we are taught to try ourselves against the principle of Virtue; checking to see if our thoughts, speech, and actions, form right angles with, or are based on, a virtuous perspective of life. The combined perspective of speculative operations shows us that we have an internal square that forever identifies when something is: right or wrong, beneficial or harmful, fair or unjust.

This is evidenced by the fact that people naturally: "sneak" to steal things; talk low when trying to deceive someone in the presence of others; or hide their faces in order to avoid being recognized while committing certain acts. This internal Square, for the initiate seeking further Light, is the true measurement of living virtuously. It serves as an internal barometer is easily ignored, and easy to override, because it is often only perceivable as a faint whisper or a "gut feeling."

Figure 5. An Egyptian Initiate seated on the Square. Notice the posture of a tried and tested Master Mason.

At this point, we can see that the three working tools of the FC are all used to determine the straightness and correctness of angles and the upright nature of a Man prior to being p.............. and eventually r................. The trowel, being added once we are r........, is operatively used to spread cement for joining bricks, stones, and other materials when building one singular structure from many parts (e pluribus unum – out of many, one). Speculatively, we are taught to use this tool to spread brotherly love, in order to facilitate unity amongst fellow travelers, thereby reducing the potential for strife and conflict within the Craft.

This combined outlook would help us, as MM, to recognize that there is also a living cement used to keep our physical bodies together. It is clearly recognizable in our ligaments used to tie our muscles to the bone, but what about the method by which our cells combine to form tissues? And how tissues bind to form organs? And how organs work together to form systems, and eventually entire organisms?

By claiming to be architects of our own Divine temples, we are now responsible for understanding our materials, our tools, and our plans. We have taken on the elevated status of Freemasons to live as shining examples standing erect on the horizon for all to see...What are we putting on display?

Just as the pyramids of Giza have withstood time, invasion, and intentional defacing, we too must be sure that our squares are proven, that our levels represent a true horizontal, and that our perpendiculars as measured by the plumb, report two 90 degree angles without the slightest error. And perhaps most importantly, that we spread the cement according to measure, in order that we may ensure that our entire structure is solid and without weakness or decay. One sure way to guarantee this goal is to formulate your own operative speculations.

The Meditative Mason

Jeff Menzise, Ph.D., 32°, FPS

*M*editation is an ancient concept that is practiced throughout the world, even in modern times. By definition, meditation is any process that alters the state of consciousness in order to enhance some aspect of the practitioner. Stereotypically, when we think of meditation we are often flooded with images of someone sitting cross-legged, eyes closed, with candles and incense burning in the background. This is a true depiction of *some* forms of meditation, but it definitely does not cover the vast majority of meditative practices.

Often ascribed to the cultures and spiritual traditions of India, meditation has been known to almost all civilizations and cultures on the planet from times immemorial. In many ancient texts, seekers will find that the main characters, especially those to whom great powers and achievements have been ascribed, practiced some form of meditation, be it prayer, fasting, exercising, ritual, etc.

In almost every case, this practice is what set them apart from all other characters in the stories. For example, Jesus periodically excused himself from his followers in order that he may partake in some sort of meditative process. In the ancient Kemetic (Egyptian) scriptures, meditation is symbolized whenever someone (such as Heru or Auset) communed with Tehuti (the symbol for Divine Wisdom).

Nowadays, meditation is gaining in popularity, especially in the "self-help" and "new age" groups springing up around the world. Many attempt to project negativity towards these groups by criticizing them as "navel-gazers" and lazy, however, anyone who has ever intentionally practiced any form of meditation understands the amount of work that goes into creating and maintaining such a discipline. The health benefits, both mental and physical, are currently being recognized more and more by medical doctors and psychologists around the world.

For example, certain cancer treatment facilities are setting themselves apart from others by incorporating what is commonly termed "alternative" and/or "complementary" approaches to treatment, which includes meditation. In the world of psychology, there is a relatively new, and quickly evolving, field known as "mindfulness," which is based on the Buddhist notion of meditation, and seeks to remedy and prevent many forms of mental illness.

As a meditation practitioner of more than 20 years, I can personally testify to its benefits and to the many ways that it has improved my life by: minimizing stress, increasing perceptual awareness, enhancing cognition, and by improving my ability to gain insight when attempting to understand something. Meditation does not require anything complex or difficult, nor does it require any large amount of time. It simply requires a few minutes a day (preferably in the morning when first waking up or in the evenings just prior to going to sleep). There are three basic parts to meditation: breathing, visualization/imagination, and verbal statements; each of which will be explored in the following pages.

Breathing

The first component of meditation for discussion is breathing. Breathing is one of the few automatic body functions that we can intentionally control with our will. For example, many of us go through our lives rarely ever thinking about our breath, or breathing, unless it is somehow obstructed (choking), we smell something foul or pleasant, or when it is brought to our attention (such as while reading this article). It is to our benefit that we do not have to think about breathing, just as we do not have to think about keeping our heart beating, our food digesting, etc. If these things depended on our conscious attention, many of us would have died long ago because we are too distracted by other things in life. Understanding the power of breath, ancient practitioners developed methods for consciously manipulating the breathing; yielding great benefit to the body and mind.

Take a moment and think about the last time you were afraid, angry, or experiencing any intense emotional state. Recall how your breathing changed. Think about the last time you watched a suspense thriller, notice how your breathing was literally "suspended" during those intense, climatic parts of the film. These examples demonstrate how our breathing is directly related to our emotional states. If emotions and states of consciousness influence certain rates of breathing, then certain rates of breathing should also influence emotions and states of consciousness.

Visualization/Imagination

The second part of meditation is the mental ability to visualize and/or imagine things in your mind. Each of us has the experience of "seeing" something "in our heads." We have all daydreamed and saw something in our minds that, during those moments, appeared to be absolutely real. We have also wanted something so badly that we were able to create an image in our mind of this thing, and sooner or later, it came to be.

The reverse is also true. Many of us have held images of things that we absolutely wanted to avoid at all costs, and due to our worrying about it, we had visualizations of the "what ifs" and sooner or later, it manifested itself in our reality. The ancients who mastered meditation realized the importance of this particular gift and also understood the power that it held. This is why at the very foundation of many great civilizations was a set of symbols used to guide the visualization and imagination of the people, who, like people all over the planet, are constantly going in and out of meditative trance throughout the day.

By providing a body of empowering, healthy symbols and images, great cultures helped their citizens to avoid much of the destructive aspects brought about by focusing their imaginative powers on negative things. Unfortunately, in today's world, much of our visual experience is one of hardship, pain, destruction, violence, and anxiety producing imagery, which then produces an expectation to physically experience the same.

Verbal Statements

Verbal statements used during meditation are also called affirmations or mantras. A mantra serves as a protective factor, in the same way that visualization/imagination does. It does so by occupying the mind with a pre-approved and consciously determined set of thoughts that will keep the mind from wandering to other, less desirable and perhaps dangerous thoughts. We all have experiences using mantras in moments when we are trying to focus and "make something happen."

For example, if your favorite basketball team is down by two points and they have a player at the free-throw line shooting two shots, you may find yourself saying under your breath "make it, make it, make it..." or if you are rooting for the opposing team, you may say "miss it, miss it, miss it..." Each of these are attempts to focus your mental energies towards a desired outcome. On a less mundane level, many of us have witnessed a religious person using the Rosary in Catholicism or Misbaha (prayer beads) in Islam as a means to conduct a certain number of prayers or recitation of a particular phrase, chant, or mantra.

The overall purpose for the mantra (verbal thoughts) is to occupy the verbal mind with something beneficial, or at least not harmful, in order to keep it from wandering into areas that are not in line with your current purpose. It is known and widely accepted that when in intense prayer and/or meditation, the body's energies are heightened and things are more likely to happen based on what we are focusing on. It would be counter-productive to intentionally meditate and/or pray for improved health, but occupy one's mind with verbalizations related to how bad you feel.

Using these three basic aspects of meditation, I would like to offer a simple process by which you can begin to apply meditation to your Masonic works. Lets start by establishing a particular rate of breathing. For those who are new to meditation or have health conditions that restrict them, please consult your health care practitioner before trying any exercise including this one.

First, get into a comfortable sitting or laying position. Begin to breathe slowly

in and out of your nose, if this is uncom-
fortable, breathe in through your nose
and out through your mouth. It is good to
have a balanced breath, which involves
inhaling for a certain count (3 seconds),
holding the breath for a certain count (3
seconds), and exhaling for a certain count
(3 seconds). I typically use a "4 Breaths
per Minute" technique where I inhale
for five seconds, hold my breath for five
seconds, and exhale for five seconds (1
breath = 15 seconds). [When doing advanced practices, I also hold my breath
for five seconds after each exhale, turning
this into a 3 breaths per minute cycle.]
While breathing in this manner, close your
eyes and imagine or visualize yourself
smiling and laughing. Repeat in your mind
the following statement "I am blessed and
happy in life."

This brief and seemingly simple
practice is designed to assist you in improving your appreciation for the life you
have, and is also designed to assist you
with the creation of a life that you want

to have. Enjoy-ment is having the mental-ity of enjoying life. By imagining yourself happy and laughing, your body and mind responds as if it's the case. By repeating this exercise consistently, you are likely to experience subtle, but very real, improve-ments to your perspective of, and experi-ences living, life.

As a Meditative Mason, we allow ourselves to be more efficient at receiv-ing Light. We position ourselves to re-move the ill will and negative feelings exemplified by the Three Ruffians, which ultimately led to the slaying of the Mas-ter Temple Builder H.A. This is one of the greatest hurdles for ALL Light seekers to overcome; thankfully, we have many tools to assist us in such a journey. An ancient statement learned in certain schools of initiation follows: *"Emotions Make Poor Leaders but Great Servants."* Meditating al-lows us to regain control of our emotional state, while increasing our mind's ability to meet our daily challenges. Try it for yourself. Be consistent and be thankful.

The Masonic Mind: Introduction

Jeff Menzise, Ph.D., 32°, FPS

*C*ognitively, those who have undergone Initiation should have certain advantages that, by rule, are not found abundantly amongst the non-initiated masses of people. The advantages are also seen in various and most other aspects of the individual person, including: emotionally, physically, and spiritually. This is the case because initiation is designed to increase awareness about certain aspects of yourself, as a human being. Aspects that, by becoming aware of them, offer a set of skills that directly impact how you perceive and interact with the world. Imagine a collective of people that are similarly developed; having a variety of human resources available, in highly efficient and highly effective forms. This is the trademark of high society.

In our institution of Freemasonry, it should be the same. We undergo processes that are designed to awaken and enhance certain characteristics, gifts, talents, and abilities. Through the proper application of our ritual, along with the intentional operationalization of our symbols and tools, the individual Mason, and thereby the collective of Masons, will begin to function in a superior fashion. These improvements are observable not only by the character of the Mason, but also in his ability to function in harmony with his purpose, restore balance to his person, and to be a blessing to his relations.

This series of articles is based on an individual course of study I developed while in graduate school. The course is designed to assist with using our culture (rituals, symbols, and working tools) in a manner that brings about our collective enhancement. In each article, I will present on a very specific quality, and demonstrate how our tools are designed to enhance and alter that quality. In addition to this philosophical discourse, I will include specific instructions of how to do it. I will primarily draw on the science of psychology, the science of religion, and many other points of reference to illustrate these lessons.

The articles are designed to be studied, considered deeply, reflected upon, and perhaps most importantly, tested and proven to and for yourself. I look forward to providing this service and pray that mutual benefit is gained by us all.

The Masonic Mind: The State of Peace

Jeff Menzise, Ph.D., 32°, FPS

*P*eace may be one of the most underrated gifts bestowed upon humans. The ability to be peaceful, not only in times of peace, but also in times of conflict and strife, is the true measure of character and a true demonstration of mastery and self-control. Think about the karate movies from the 1970s. In those films, the wise elder-masters would appear emotionally unshaken while battling. Because of this, their skills were far superior to any contender who approached them from a place of emotion.

In our daily lives we are presented with many opportunities to exercise our right to be peaceful: in our relationships, our workspace, with our family, and amongst our Bredren and Sistren in the Lodge. The importance of maintaining peace cannot be overstated. There are many proven benefits to our mental, social, and physical well-being.

Psychologists have identified the impact of stress (the lack of peace) on our ability to think clearly, recall information, articulate our thoughts to others, and even to make sound decisions. We have all personally experienced how being "stressed out" can negatively impact our interactions with friends and loved ones.

A stressed-out person typically has a lower tolerance for others. They are more likely to respond with harshness, and disproportional levels of anger and frustration when "annoyed." No one enjoys the presence of such a person; they may be tolerated based on some degree of dependency, but they are rarely desired.

Regarding our physical health and well-being, the lack of peace and the presence of stress presents major issues.

Heart disease, diabetes, digestive trouble, weakened immunity, obesity, kidney disease, asthma, chronic pain, and even some cancers are known to proliferate as a result of an excessively stressful disposition. This is why stress is known as "the silent killer." It is the underlying fuel that maintains and increases the destructive nature of many physical and psychological ailments. In a study of stress in the United Kingdom, researchers found that approximately 13.4 million work days were lost due, in part, to stress. This impacts overall productivity as well as one's ability to care for themselves and their family.

Unfortunately, due to covert and overt experiences with racism and race-based discrimination here in the United States, the environment is full of potential stress for our Prince Hall Family. Fortunately for us, we have our community of Freemasons and Eastern Stars, and all the wonderful tools we have received while become Stars and Masons, to assist us in maintaining our peace; even in the face of hardship. One such tool as found in our ritual and ceremony is the *Rite of Enlightenment,* or the intellectual enlightenment "that indicates the triumphant conclusion of man's conflicts." The truly enlightened Mason is fully capable of utilizing our V of SL, one of the three G. L., to find guidance for navigating and negotiating life experiences in a way that is beneficial to their well-being, with minimal negative stress.

The enlightened Mason is able to look upon the symbols of the square, level, and plumb, and understand the value of living harmoniously with ourselves and each other, practicing equality by living the "Golden Rule," and living a just and upright life. In our more ancient symbols, found amongst the Egyptian iconography, we find the scales of Maat in the judgment scene. Here we have the initiate's heart being weighed against the feather of truth, righteousness, reciprocity, and justice. The heart should balance out, meaning, there should be neither excess nor deficiency when it comes to living truth.

Balance should be sought in both praise and punishment.

These symbols are easily applied to our interactions with others, however, we often have difficulty when it comes to applying them to ourselves. Our ancient predecessors identified the worst type of violation to be the ones made against yourself. So, if we are not taking care of ourselves, our personal relationship with our own body, mind, and spirit, but are making our rounds in the Lodge, doing everything for everybody else, we are committing a great crime against ourselves.

Without self-care, we leave ourselves vulnerable to stress, and all of the negative outcomes of such an experience. The key is to "live in peace," long before we have to "rest in peace." This peace will allow us to honor the true length of our cable-tows. It will allow us to honor the 24-inch gauge. And perhaps most importantly, it will provide the stability of a smooth and perfect ashlar upon which to rest the temple we are continually constructing.

The Masonic Mind:
The Charge

Jeff Menzise, Ph.D., 32°, FPS

"*B*e diligent, prudent, temperate, discreet." This admonishment is given to every Master Masons as a reminder of how we are to live our daily lives as we move from the Lodge into the "outer world." As a dutiful Mason, we are encouraged to exhibit these traits at all times and in all places, both when dealing with our fellow Brothers, and with the uninitiated masses. Consistently displaying these virtues helps to "build the brand" of Freemasonry as a Craft that produces and has as its membership, Men who are leaders, Men who are responsible, Men who are mature, Men who are virtuous, Men who are strong, Men who are wise,

Men who are organized, Men who are for-ward-thinking, Men who are serious, Men who are focused, Men who are respect-able and respectful, Men who are depend-able, Men who are measured, Men who are intentional, Men who are thorough... Good Men, Made Better.

Let us further our understanding of this Charge by defining each word and seeing how we can practically apply them in the "real world."

Diligent

To be diligent is to have or show care and conscientiousness in one's work or duties. Showing care and being consci-entious are typical qualities of a person who sees value in what they are doing, and who sees value in the people who are impacted by their actions and presence. The conscientious Man is one that takes pride in the outcome of their actions, and therefore are usually mindful in their ap-proach, circumspect in their perspectives, and generous in charity. Diligence as a virtue is what makes relationships strong, people trustworthy, and organizations thrive.

Prudent

To be prudent is to act with, or show, care and thought for the future. Very closely related to diligence, prudence takes the benefits of diligence and applies it towards the future. As builders, it should be part of every plan to make sure, from the outset, that the structure will stand firmly in the end. Our ancient African Bredren perfectly demonstrate this in the many monuments that have stood immovable for thousands of years. To have a future-oriented mind is to have a mind that sees beyond the present moment, beyond the current step, and beyond the immediate situation.

The prudent mind is a mind that time-travels in order to envision the outcomes, and to make the necessary modifications in the here-and-now, in order to ensure that the tomorrow they have seen, actually arrives. Our Founding Fifteen were absolutely prudent in their approach to erecting African Lodge #1 and seeking a Charter for what would eventually become African Lodge #459. The social justice leanings of our Brotherhood are never oriented to the present alone; no, they are very much intended to pave a smoother path for our future generations. The attribute of prudence is sewn into every sunset and guarantees that light will shine anew in the morning.

Temperate

To be temperate is to show moderation or self-restraint. This level of self-discipline is required if one is to persevere in trying times, overcome obstacles and avoid snares and traps along the way. The untempered soul is often wayward; easily manipulated by unseen forces like a leaf blown by the wind. The drunkard and addicted person betrays the lack of temperance, and demonstrates the costly condition brought about by an inability or an unwillingness to tame our passions. Passions are always seductive, and often come subtle in their approach; manipulating situations and circumstances to make our choosing experiences that contradict our best interests, an easy decision to be made.

Self-restraint is paramount in the seeking of Light mostly because of the strength of ignorance, and how strongly our old ways cling to our life-force, and fight for our attention. For example, the person who decides to give up smoking awakens the heretofore dormant fighting-spirit of smoking. The person who decides to modify their diet by giving up red meat, almost summons "the gods red-meat" to come and test them, forcing them to prove their word. There are people who have declared that they would no longer eat candy, only to find an absolutely free box of candy being offered to them. To dare to claim growth and refinement as a part of one's intentions, requires that we first develop temperance, if we hope to be successful, and capable of enduring the inevitable tests.

Discreet

To be discreet is to be careful and circumspect in one's speech and/or actions, especially in order to avoid causing offense or gaining an undeserved advantage. This is purely a skill of the tongue, which is often used to move others to action, or is itself activated in order to prevent oneself from having to act. Our ancient Ancestors of Egypt (Kemet) referred to this as the "weighing of words," and found it a necessary discipline if one is to successfully navigate this world and the next. Intentional speech and action, measured words and steps, often denotes a strategic movement as opposed to a spontaneous and reactionary, ill-thought plan.

The use of discretion is what creates opportunities for success, in that it tailor makes what others are able to perceive of you and your character. It avoids

60

offense by a careful study of that which may be considered offensive; it creates opportunities for advancement by demonstrating a careful nature, one that may be trusted with valuable knowledge and/or possessions. The lack of discretion, in both speech and action, has sunk many ships; while the ability to uphold this virtue has built and sustained long-lasting institutions like our beloved organization of Freemasonry.

Take heed my Brothers to the directive heretofore explained. Be sure to spend ample amounts of time reflecting upon these words and see to it that you strive to implement some aspect of them into your daily life. It is up to us to maintain the image and substance of Freemasonry because we are the ones who have chosen to do so. It is our charge to take care of our reputation, and to understand that we are always representing what it means to be a Mason. How do you measure up?

The Masonic Mind: For the Future

Jeff Menzise, Ph.D., 32°, FPS

"We should understand that what we do today, is not for ourselves, but for our future generations. If we adopt this idea and attitude as we work our Craft, we will slowly but surely begin to see the effects in our children and grandchildren. We will once again be giant pillars in our communities, shining Light for all to see and emulate. It is within reach, and worth the effort it will take to close the gap."

- Jeff Menzise, Symbolically Speaking Vol. 1, African Lodge #1 – The Context

*A*s a principle of time, the present moment carries the imperative of life. The past is spent, the future being sown. Spent is not "gone," and being sown does not mean "not here yet." The present moment is an extension of the past moment; a direct derivative. Similar to mitosis (cell division), time replicates itself with the potential for metamorphosis and mutation. Your daily experiences alter the "DNA" of time for your particular, individual, and specific life experience, thereby sowing the seeds of your future.

"Time spent" is a transformative process that evolves almost all things subject to time's influence. That means everything that has ever happened, known and unknown, has some form of influence over everything and all things that are going on right now, both known and unknown. This is a very powerful notion because it identifies the power of the present moment. It is currency. You pay "now," for what you get next, which means the "now" being cultivated, is altering the value of your exchange with life. Paradoxically, what you have now, is what you could afford to buy in the previous moment. Meditate on this concept, deeply.

With this understanding ever-developing within the Masonic Mind, we eventually arrive at a point of co-existing: yesterday, today, and tomorrow. We begin to realize and experience the Omnipresence, or ever-present aspect, of the GAOTU. Time traveling literally becomes a possibility. You are able to clearly project your mind and awareness to any point in time, with various levels of clarity. I know this may sound "deep," or "out there," however, I ask that you bear with me for a few as I attempt to make it plain by example.

Take a moment and think about what you were doing right before you picked up this book and began reading. Did you sit down? Did you get a drink? Whatever it was, take a moment and think about it, imagining as much detail as possible. This is time traveling to the past. The more focused and empowered your mind, the greater your ability to experience and utilize this tool. Similarly, you can travel to the future, using the same tool; visualizing and imagining, in great detail, what it is you desire to experience. Keep focused and active in your pursuit (active meaning actively choosing to be passive or active in this pursuit). This will lead you to exactly what you imagined and willed.

This can be both empowering and potentially intimidating at the same time. Realizing that we have the ability to intentionally learn from our past, to better comprehend our present, which in turn, helps us to better plan for the future, empowers us to be the creators of our reality. When it comes to our future generations, this capability, if consciously employed, ensures that we build an ironclad system and organization within which our children and grandchildren find the guidance, protection, and knowledge required for them to successfully navigate this rapidly changing world.

There are several of our Masonic symbols that speak directly to the power and influence of time. These symbols are the tools we will need to make this effort as efficient and effective as possible. Over the next few articles, I will begin to decode some of our symbols focusing specifically on how they can be used to influence both our understanding of time, as well as our ability to manipulate it in our own favor.* It is my hope that this series will prove beneficial to our working of the Craft as descendants of African Lodge #1, and that it will provide the necessary insight to help us to build for a brighter tomorrow. Remember, what we do now is not for us, but for our future generations.

*These articles are included in Volume 1 of the Masonic Meditation Series.

Ritual

Jeff Menzise, Ph.D., 32°, FPS

*W*hat if Prince Hall, and the other fourteen founding Brothers, fully intended for us to recognize and utilize an African understanding of Freemasonry while practicing our Craft? What if we left everything the *way* it is, and simply shifted our perspective and understanding of *what* it is? What if we viewed our various rituals from an African worldview and perspective? What if we collectively understood ritual to be a tool for bringing together the various aspects of reality (social, personal, divine), melding them into one total experience?

This perspective of ritual would ultimately serve to expand one's understanding of the sacred, in order to encompass ALL aspects of experience, making everything in everyday life, a symbolic expression of limitless truth and an opportunity to commune with the divine. And thus, we'd return power to our practice.

Instead, many adopt the Western view of ritual, which isolates it within proscribed boundaries, limiting it to certain times, days, and settings...and thus the "holy" and so-called "secular" are made separate and are given room to exist as individual realities. This segregative notion of ritual and reality is what allows for the removal of sacredness from various aspects of life, leaving institutions and individuals vulnerable to the infectious agents of baseness and banality. It's the very thinking that rationalizes and formulates excuses for the "pedophile man of the cloth" who attempts to fulfill his sick cravings on his unsuspecting congregation.

According to Evan Zuesse[1], and what he calls the "ritual vision of life":

---

1   See *Ritual Cosmos: The Sanctification of Life in African Religions*, p. 9.

Ritual itself is concerned first of all with
ordering bodily movements in space,
and clearly the body is the foundation
for all awareness. But ritual not only
provides for classifications of bodily,
social and especially cosmic space, it
also seeks to interrelate these spheres in
a harmonious and fruitful manner, so as
to transform and renew the universe.

This understanding identifies another very important purpose for ritual, the
lofty goal of transforming and renewing the
universe. For the initiate, the constant participation in ritual helps to strengthen their
understanding of the universe while simultaneously equipping them with the necessary
knowledge and practical skills to produce
harmony within their respective worlds (internal and external).

We are currently functioning under
a very limited understanding of science and
knowledge. The current paradigm is highly externalized and very much dependent
on materialism for both evidence of Truth
and comforts. If only we understood that

our ability to "know," and knowledge itself, both exist well beyond what is currently referred to as *the* scientific method[2], and that our Light can shine exponentially brighter simply by shifting perspective. But what are the methods used to make this shift? What are these ritual practices? And how does one cultivate and develop them? I'm glad you asked. These questions and many more will be explored throughout this article.

The internal and external tools available to an African initiate are many. Their accessibility depends upon the degree of initiation, and they manifest uniquely in each individual. Amongst the repertoire of tools are: intuition, direct knowing, mind

---

2   I emphasize "the" because many erroneously believe it to be the one and only way to know and utilize science. It is, in fact, only "a" scientific method, one of many that are equally valid. Evidence of a scientific method beyond the one currently used by modern science is found in Western science's inability to understand how the many ancient pyramids were built, and their inability to duplicate it. Much in the same way that modern science cannot "create" life.

over matter, telepathy, telekinesis, prophecy, foresight, foreknowledge, etc. These tools are commonly lumped into the somewhat "conspiratorial" category of extra-sensory perception, or ESP. The thing about ESP is many people misunderstand what it is, and thus believe it to be some sort of spooky pseudo-science. This couldn't be farther from the truth. ESP by definition is the ability to perceive without the use of the known physical senses, or in a way that exceeds the current understanding of these senses.

Making it more plain, ESP is when you had a "hunch" to do something and it proved to be beneficial. It's when "something" told you to call someone, go somewhere, or stay at home, and as a result, proved beneficial. The converse is also true: the thought "crosses" your mind to do something or be somewhere but you *don't* follow through, learning later that if you had, it would have benefited you. Have you ever been thinking of someone or something and it shows up either in a commercial, conversation, or the person calls, texts, or otherwise makes contact with you? That too, is ESP[3].

Now of course there are times when one has actually "sensed" something and was not aware of having seen, heard, smelled, tasted, or touched it; this is separate from ESP. This is simply unconscious sensing, or sensing beneath the threshold of conscious awareness. The way to hone, develop and cultivate these talents is similar to how one would develop themselves physically, via exercise and practice. There are two basic vehicles for exercising these mental and spiritual "muscles": ritual and symbolism.

By Western definition, a ritual is: 1) an established or prescribed procedure for a religious or other rite; 2) a system or collection of religious or other rites; 3) observance of set forms in public worship; 4) a book of rites or ceremonies; 5) a book containing the offices to be used by priests in administering

---

3   There is a well-established body of academic research into the mechanisms of ESP and its various manifestations. See *New Frontiers of the Mind - The Story of the Duke [University] Experiments* and *The Reach of the Mind* by J. B. Rhine.

the sacraments and for visitation of the sick, burial of the dead, etc.; 6) a prescribed or established rite, ceremony, proceeding, or service; and, 7) prescribed, established, or ceremonial acts or features collectively, as in religious service. These definitions pale in comparison to the one offered at the opening of this article; it seems to lack the depth of the African perspective.

On the surface, they describe ritual as a standard and regular way of doing things. We also see that the term can refer to a written description of the various stations within a group, including their roles and responsibilities. Additionally, many of these definitions refer to some sort of religious organization or ceremonial rites, or the book containing a description of these ceremonial rites. So, from the Western perspective, ritual is a step-by-step process; a way of ensuring uniformity, consistency, and establishes familiarity; in other words, it is formulaic.

From an African perspective, the consistency, and prescribed methodology is there, however, there simultaneously exists the understanding that the ritual goes beyond the formula; in fact, it exists *for the purpose of* going beyond the *formula* (i.e., the physical boundaries of reality). The processes, scripts, songs/sounds, required movements, scents, colors, etc., *all* serve as ritualistic tools; they are the forms through which the actual work is being done. It's similar to how the amount of water in a crystal wine glass, coupled with the shape and density of the crystal, produces the range of sounds one gets by plucking it or running their finger around the rim. In other words, its movement (vibration) is manipulated by its physical make-up. The sound is the true work, while the glass and water represent the form(ula) through which the work takes place. Try hard to visualize and understand this concept, because it is key to looking deeper into, and broadening our understanding of, how powerful Masonic ritual could actually be, when approached from the African worldview.

It is true that the work gets done with or without our knowing what is being done.

And thus, a person can listen to a symphony and be emotionally moved by the harmonics, and may even develop lucidity of thought, all the while not understanding a thing about the relationship between music, cognition, and emotions. On the other hand, the person who is consciously aware of this relationship is capable of employing this knowledge to their own benefit. They can consciously establish intention and approach the symphony prepared to take full advantage of the opportunity, coming with a particular problem in mind, about which they wish and expect to gain clarity and insight through the course of the performance.

This is intuitively, and perhaps instinctively, done by people everyday. For example, people choose a certain music for the sole purpose of altering their own mood and/or that of another. People have certain music they use to exercise, to relax, to become aroused or otherwise set the mood, increase mental focus and clarity, etc. These are all examples of how music is used in an everyday manner, for ritualistic purposes.

Now, imagine this mental and emotionally manipulative tool being intentionally employed for the purpose of spiritual self-development. In essence, that is the function of religious hymns and chants. They are tools for manipulating thoughts, emotions, and behaviors. It's the reason why in movies, the music often shifts to some sort of "hip hop-ish" beat when the scene switches to a "dangerous" or otherwise "urban" environment. It sets the tone for how you will feel watching that scene, and in similar environments in real life.

This same level of subtle influence is found throughout society and especially in our religious institutions. The masses fail to realize that everything from the songs they sing to the construction of the house of worship (church, temple, lodge, synagogue, etc.), create the experiences they have while in attendance. Without knowledge of this fact, the participant may still receive some benefit, yet, based on their lack of intentionality when it comes to using the tools present during the ritual, they are unlikely to take full advantage.

It's similar to the ever-growing features found on smart phones. Between the "apps" and the hardware, these pocket computers can impact almost every thinkable thing that people do on a day-to-day basis. Let's say a person has 5,000 features on their phone but they are only aware of and only use the call feature. Sure they are able to accomplish a lot with this single tool, however, they have come no where near maximizing the potential of the device.

Compare this to the possibilities once they learn to text, browse the internet, take pictures, record videos, produce music, produce movies, play any number of games, shine a flashlight, pay bills, invest money, learn a language, etc., etc., etc., all from the same device. Their world and life experiences will become totally different, perhaps expanded, or maybe even contracted. This phenomenal and life altering difference is exactly what we find between the person who intentionally recognizes and uses ritual, beyond the surface motions and outward expressions, and those who maintain a limited, concrete and superficial understanding.

In exploring the concept of ritual further, we will go both deeper and more superficially in order to cover its mundane and spiritual aspects. It is important for us to discuss both extremes in order to develop a well-rounded understanding of ritual, its power, as well as its familiarity and accessibility. By the time we finish with this article, our comprehension of ritual should be expanded and we should understand that everything we do can be ritualized, and thus, can possess the power to transform.

On the mundane or surface level, we participate in rituals without needing to think about it. From the way we wake up, to how we go to bed, we are constantly performing some task in a set, consistent and prescribed way. Think about what you do when you first wake up. Do you typically pray upon rising? Do you drink a glass of lemon water? Brush teeth? Shower? Exercise? Meditate? Whatever your morning routine, it is a ritual. In some schools of thought, the morning ritual is what sets the tone for the remainder of the day, hence the saying "woke up on the wrong side of the bed." This conveys that something was off in the morning ritual, and thus, has negatively affected the rest of the day.

Once awake, people tend to continue in ritualistic fashion. We typically eat breakfast in a consistent manner; some have a cup of coffee and read the paper, others make smoothies. Children may have a bowl of cereal while watching cartoons and/or reading the cereal box. Our morning commute is really no different. We typically travel the same way, be it on public transportation (bus, train, taxi) or personal vehicle, this routine also comes with its ritual, and consists of various elements like: road rage, crowds, smells, traffic, radio programs, and sometimes the stress of being early, on time, or late.

Once we arrive at our destination, we continue to ritualize. Do you open the office? Do you have to change into uniform? Do you open and read email? Check phone messages? Have a morning staff meeting? Again, this is all ritual. It is a set routine or mode of operating. It contributes to how you function and how you experience your workplace and job. Your co-workers and clients are co-players in your ritual, contributing whatever they bring from their wake up and early morning rituals too. In these public spaces, ritual can easily become a tricky pot of gumbo with a little bit of everything thrown into it. This can be distracting, confusing, or fantastically beneficial, all depending on what the people are bringing, and perhaps more importantly, your preparation and how you view what is taking place around you.

Once our workplace rituals have concluded, we typically return to the commuter phase: sometimes it is simply the reverse of our morning travels, other times it may come with its own special nuances. Some people habitually go to happy hour after work, some times everyday, sometimes on a specific day of the week (when their favorite restaurant or bar offers drink specials). Some will stop by the grocery store or market in order to pick up food to prepare for dinner once they get home. You may have to pick up kids from a day care center or school; there may be evening meetings or conferences you have to attend. One main difference between the morning and evening commute (or vice versa depending on if you work in the mornings or nights), is you typically are more energetic going in than you are coming back, having expended your mental and physical energies at work.

Finally, we have our night time ritual. We typically use this time to wind-down, prepare for bed, cook dinner, watch television, and spend time with our families. Just like the previous steps, this phase is also full of specific experiences and procedures. Take a moment and think about what you did last night before going to bed. Did you brush your teeth? Did you iron your clothes for the next day? Did you prep dinner? Eat while sitting in the same seat you always sit in? Watch your favorite TV shows? Help a child with their homework? Browse social media? Was this consistent with the night before? I'm betting it was consistent in more ways than not. Humans tend to be creatures of habit, and thus, we readily lend ourselves to participating in and benefiting from ritual.

We can take this same concept and apply it to our exercise routines. Do you wear specific clothes to workout? Do you go to a specific gym? Start with a particular machine or muscle group? Carry a special water bottle? I'm betting you do. The same goes for our sexual and intimate lives, where we also typically have rituals that we perform. Folks may take a shower, drink some wine, put on some sensual music, dress a certain way, use a particular oil or perfume, prepare special dishes, take sexual enhancement supplements, etc.

The actual sex act tends to also be routine for many. You start with the same act, move to a particular position, and if you are lucky, you get a few more positions in, then climax. After which, is the "clean up" where folks use the bathroom, take showers, put on clothes, and if you're at home, go to sleep, if not, you go home. Whatever your routine, if it is routine, it is ritual.

The main thing that takes our ritual participation from being superficial to a more in-depth process, is our intention behind the routine. What do we intend to accomplish? What is our understanding of how our mind, body, and spirit all participate in each of these activities? How are we benefited, mind, body, and spirit by participating in these daily routines? If, for any of these tasks, we say there is no benefit to mind, body, and spirit, then we are only dealing superficially.

I tend to place some of our more intentional rituals like funerals, births, and weddings, at the mid-point between the superficial and the deepest of ritual practices. These events naturally carry a more obvious sense of sacredness because they serve as clear points of transition in our lives. When a person is expecting a child, we intuitively know that this is a powerful and divine process. Of course we don't always consciously and overtly acknowledge this fact, nonetheless, we feel it. From the non-ritualistic standpoint, the process of birth, for many, entails an unplanned conception, a medically-based pregnancy, and a hospitalized birth. In modern times, this is the norm. Technology has "advanced" to such a point that we are now capable of selecting our child's birth date (within a certain range), and scheduling the delivery of your child with as much confidence as you would place an order with your local pizzeria.

Remember, anything that is routine is also ritual. In the case of the hospitalized birth, the medical staff also functions based on a ritual. They will even call it a "routine procedure." Their process is complete with consistent visits and checkups, each of which carries its own specific protocol. Expecting mothers are advised to carry on in a certain way, following certain protocols including prenatal vitamins, birthing classes, and the development of a birthing plan.

When labor occurs (either naturally or medically induced) the mother will either experience a natural vaginal birth or cesarean section (C-section). In the former, the attending medical staff will constantly check the cervix to measure how far it has dilated. They will also determine the position of the baby to see if it is in proper form (head down, facing backwards), or in one of the breach positions (sitting up facing forward with legs crossed or loose). Each of these variations determines what protocol to follow.

Regardless of the method, most women that give birth, and their families that witness it, see it as a miracle. Women have described it as being indescribable. The process of pregnancy, where a woman actually grows another person inside of her own body, gives women a direct experience of God. The moment that the developing fetus awakens in her womb, and moves for the first time, solidifies the miracle in her heart and mind. The flashes of communication, understanding and knowing that a mother shares with the child in her womb, is how God must feel with each of us.

That moment when the baby is born, and the mother meets and touches him or her for the first time, is like a reunion of long lost relatives who play catch-up for the remainder of their lives. In some African cultures, this relationship is exactly that; the child is understood to be a returning Ancestor, while the parents are also relatives from times long ago. When one makes their transition (dies), they continue in the cycle of familial relationships, and thus, the circle remains unbroken.

This relatively new process of "medicalized" birth can easily take away from the deeper ritualistic aspects previously associated with birth. In ancient times, and still amongst those who carry on tradition, this process was governed by a midwife who is likely to have learned her craft from an elder, more experienced midwife, who has likely been initiated into the mystical sciences of life and giving birth.

From this perspective, birth, as a ritual, begins with conception. Ideally, this occurs between two people who have undergone training and preparation to become the healthiest and most capable woman and man they can be. Having gone through their respective rites of passage/initiations, the man and woman thus joined in matrimony, would ritualize sex, ritualize conception, ritualize pregnancy, ritualize birth, and ritualize the raising of that child.

According to Simon Ottenberg in ***Boyhood Rituals in an African Society, An Interpretation***:

> The baby is born onto the ground. It should cry; this is taken as a sign of health and vitality...When the placenta appears the umbilical cord is cut by the midwife or another female. The child is then rubbed with sand to wash it, or often nowadays with soap and water. The skin is smoothed with palm oil and white chalk is put on it. The chalk cools the skin and it is also employed at Afikpo as a multivocal symbol of good health, fertility, good life, and happiness. The placenta and cord are buried in the courtyard—a practical procedure which also connects the child with the spirits of the ground, *ale*, associated with human welfare and fertility. The mother bathes in a special solution of water in which certain

leaves have been soaked. A secret ritual is performed over the child by the women present. I could find no male who knew it, nor did any female inform me of what it was about. Men are forbidden to view it. The rite differs according to the infant's sex; and so begins the lifelong recognition of the importance of gender and of secrecy at Afikpo.

As revealed by the author, the ritual aspects of birth are secret and are entrusted only to those who have been initiated into these rites. This is how serious we once took ourselves. Fortunately, there still exist those who acknowledge the sanctity of conception, gestation, and birth. Many still use midwives and have "home-births," "water-births," and otherwise ritualized births. People continue in the traditions of their Ancestors as much as practically possible. There are even those who go the medicalized route, and still maintain their awareness of the sacredness of the ritual taking place.

Both of my children were born to ritual. In one case we were with an African-centered organization with initiated priestesses present along with a midwife. In the other case, we also ritualized, but this time my wife and I were the priest and priestess and the midwife was one of European descent, who had been initiated (formally or not) into her Craft, specializing in the natural delivery of babies that are in breach position. During this particular pregnancy, we consulted several Oracle systems[4] and were able to identify that there would be an unexpected occurrence with this delivery.

We checked the Oracle to see the most beneficial place and method for us to have our child. We had our preferences, but the Oracle advised against each and every one of them. It told us to visit *The Farm* in Summertown, TN. At the time, this was about a 2-hour drive from our house.

The midwives at this farm are the au-

---

4   In the speech by John T. Hilton quoted in the Foreword of Symbolically Speaking, vol 1, he endorses, in true African fashion, the use of Oracles, "Let us be directed to that sure and invariable guide, the divine Oracles of God..."

thors and contributors of the popular book *Spiritual Midwifery*, and are among the few who would dare to deliver a "breach" baby, naturally (meaning vaginally, without drugs or C-section). At the time of our consultations with the Oracles, we did not know that our baby would come breach. We did know that we were being guided to this particular group for the safe and healthy delivery of our child. During labor, as things began to intensify, my wife and I went into a mutual ritual space, within our conjoined souls, and began to call on all of the female deities of our Ancestors, and we called on all of the women who have successfully walked this path before us, in order that we may draw on their strength and support during this difficult and potentially dangerous process.

When it came time for the midwife to bring our baby's head out from the womb (in a breach birth, the head is the last part to come out...so imagine a full body up to the chin extending from the womb), the room was absolutely silent. You could feel the energies being drawn into the midwife as she took on a sort of blank and entranced gaze. She was calling on her source of wisdom for this most important part of the birth. She suddenly, and with one swift movement, reached in with her fingers in a scooping motion and brought our child completely into this world. We finalized this part of the ritual with the cleansing waters from our tears of joy. We continued to ritualize for our children by divining their purpose for being born, and subsequently naming them based on this purpose[5].

Marriage is another ritualized process that many still hold with some level of sanctity. Most perform the ceremony in the presence of family members and other important individuals. There is hardly a wedding ceremony that does not include someone who is considered to be a "holy" woman or man officiating. These ceremonies often occur in a place of worship or some natural

---

5   According to many African traditions, the naming is what reminds the child and community of the person's life purpose. See *African Names* by Hehi Metu Ra Enkhamit.

setting, both of which are designed to inspire a feeling of God's presence as witness to this "holy matrimony."

The importance of this union is understood and is conveyed by the vows claiming to stay together until "death do you part." The marriage of man and woman serves as the foundation of the new family-to-be. It is from this union that new life is generated, families formed, and the human race continued.

In relatively modern times, people have begun to spend enormous amounts of money for elaborate and beautiful marriage rituals. For example, the typical wedding in the United States costs between $19,833 and $33,055, not including the honeymoon. The average American marriage lasts about 8 years before divorce, with divorce rates improving slightly and marriage rates decreasing.

Statistically speaking, women file for the majority of divorces, albeit for various reasons ranging from sexual dissatisfaction to abuse. Some contribute the preponderance of failed marriages, high cost of weddings, and declining instances of matrimony, to the increased exposure to fantasy-romance found in children's cartoons and movies. These media often provide an unrealistic expectation of romance and imagery of what "good" relationships are, to the point that folks either mistake courting, and all the bliss associated with it, to mean "real love" OR, they mistake the lack of "fairy tale" experiences to mean that love does not exist.

The African-centered perspective of marriage is one that goes beyond the sometimes superficially based notions found in Western societies. Instead of the romantic notions of "love," people who share the African-centered worldview often see matrimony as a means for cultivating and experiencing unconditional love. The African-centered perspective sees marriage as the uniting of two families, as opposed to two individuals coming together. To go a step further, beyond uniting two families, they are also uniting two bloodlines, two lineages, both of which trace all the way back to the most ancient of Ancestors, God. In essence, the marriage of man and woman reconciles the separation we experienced, from God, during our creation process, as outlined in the majority of the world's great religions.

The reunification of these complementary aspects of God, via marriage, in an African-centered community, begins with the conception and birthing rituals outlined above. It continues with the rites of passage initiations experienced by children as they approach adolescence, and then from adolescence to adulthood. Another amazing observation of non-Western perspectives on marriage is that many cultures actually see the current union as a continuation of previous relationships, which have existed from the beginning of time, amongst the various generations of Ancestors.

Perhaps one of the most profound aspects of marriage from an African-centered perspective is the notion that it has a divine purpose for the individuals involved. This purpose being to once again realize and actualize their divine nature. This is done through the work that will inevitably arise as two people become intertwined in holy matrimony, especially in ritual, in front of God, the Ancestors, and their families. I have often jokingly stated that it is a cruel joke for us to have to work out ALL of our "baggage" with the same person we are supposed to unconditionally love and grow with. It also makes the absolute most sense!

Think for a moment, about all of the time we spend with our spouses and those we are in relationships with. This person sees you beyond the dressed up, smelling good, looking good, sounding good, feeling good, "public person" you appear to be, to the less intimate people in your life. They know what your morning breath and "number 2" smell like. They know you when you are sick and when you have a bad attitude. They see you without the latest fashions and know your hygiene styles and habits.

This is enough for anyone to break up with another person with whom they have not made a deep, marriage commitment. This is the person whom you vent to, the person who must experience your work-based stress along with you. This person is also the one with whom you may generate your own feelings of stress, burden, disagreement and frustrations, in addition to all the other things that have already been spelled out. This is separate from the other energies that come with having children, and growing older. As you can probably see, marriage from a Western perspective does not equip individuals to undertake such a task with any measure of success and happiness. From the African-centered perspective, we gain a measure of hope.

According to Ra Un Nefer Amen in his book ***An Afrocentric Guide To A Spiritual Union***:

> The consummation of the wedding takes place at a ceremony which may take place anywhere from several weeks to over a year after the consent has been given. An important part in preparing for the marriage is the families getting to know each other, the education of the couples, improvement of the girl's health through

enhanced nutrition as she is prepared for pregnancy, and the groom's efforts to raise the dowry. It is important to realize that the difference between the African dowry versus the European resides in the fact that in the latter the woman brings it to the man, while in the former man brings it, not to the woman, but to her father and family. While in the European version, it can be construed as a token that one may give to another for showing favor towards one, the African dowry is more like a bond...To raise the dowry, they have to be in good social standing—an important quality that the dowry system was invented to test. A boy of good social standing would have no problem getting help from his uncles...father, married sisters, cousins, grand parents, and the boys of his age set (this is the group of boys with whom he underwent his Rites of Passage, and share other social responsibilities)...This dowry will thus act as a potent force to pressure the married couple to do right in the marriage, for the faulted party in the event of divorce would forfeit the dowry.

Once married, the husband is expected to spend more of his time with his uncles, father, and older men, than with his wife, and the wife is expected to spend more time with her mother, aunts, and older women than with her husband. In fact, it is customary for them to keep separate households. This expectation, which carries the force of law, which is to say that they cannot circumvent it, accomplishes several things. For one, it physically cuts back on the possibility of sexual overindulgence, and for another, it forces the young married couple into a situation which will guarantee their education into manhood and woman-hood. You just can't give information on the subject, however scholarly, and expect it to take root in the behavior of the majority of people. You have to have [a] means of inculcating it. Since a man cannot learn how to be a husband and fa-ther from his wife, he has to be made to spend the appropriate time with the only ones who can teach him that—successful husbands and fathers. The same is true of women. Their husbands cannot teach them how to become wives and mothers.

They must be made to spend the required time with their mothers, and aunts. Unlike western wives and husbands who expected each other to share and solve the emotional heavies that can come along in life, in spite of their lack of preparation and experience, the African couple knew to place such burdens on their more experienced relatives.

In line with the above, I experienced an aspect of the African perspective and practice of wedding two people. Back in 1999, while in Gambia, West Africa, I was blessed and fortunate to participate in a wedding ceremony of two good friends who also traveled from the U.S. The ceremony was held in an African compound in full tradition. As we sat observing the ceremony we all received a shock when the officiating elder suddenly stopped the ceremony and proclaimed that the couple could not be married because the groom had not produced the required dowry. The audience went into a fuss.

The American Africans present were

distraught because apparently no one was told of this custom beforehand. Instinct kicked in for me and one other friend as we began to go around and collect money from everyone our friend had invited. Putting my own money into the pot, I walked over to the officiating elder and asked if this was satisfactory and if they could now continue with their ceremony. Without counting the money, the elder accepted the offer and continued the service. In hindsight, I realize, as outlined above, the dowry was not to pay for any specific thing, nor was it necessary to have any specific amount, but only to show that he was, in fact, in good standing and that his community of friends and family had his back. Two babies and fifteen years later, they remain happily married.

The third level of ritual I'd like to acknowledge are those that are fully intentional ceremonies, designed to, and fully expected to, have an impact on the mind, body, and spirit of the participants. These are our religious services including: weekly church meetings, Catholic Mass, Islamic Jumu'ah, the Bah'ai services, Egbe of the Ifa groups, Akom of the Akan, monthly full moon rituals of the Ausar Auset Society, etc.

In our mainstream experience, we have various levels of intensity and intentionality that these rituals bring to the practitioner, and thus we have differing outcomes. For example, we have witnessed scenes from a Pentecostal ritual where the participants are deep into trance, handling snakes, and perhaps speaking in tongue. We have witnessed the solemn Catholic rituals where the priests are swinging the thurible[6], singing in low tones, deep in prayer. Some of us have felt the chills associated with the Islamic call to prayer, beautifully sang over the loud speaker for all the town to hear. Many of us have even experienced first-hand, in a Baptist church, where the organ accompanying the preacher's voice, is capable of bringing certain members of the congregation to such a frenzy that "Church Mothers" dance and whirl about, totally possessed with the Holy

---

6   An incense holder (censer) suspended on a chain.

Spirit.

 I recall a story once shared with me about a particular church experience. There was a congregant who was known to be susceptible to being "possessed" by the Holy Spirit. This particular elder would get possessed, slide down from her pew onto the floor, and slide all the way down to the front of the church, going under each pew in front of her. The congregants came to expect this occurrence and prepared themselves accordingly by picking up their bags and whatever else may be in her path in order to keep their stuff from being dragged down to the altar with the "possessed" Elder.

 Many who participate in this level of ritual do so with intention but without a sense of personal power. We often go to church, the mosque, the temple, with a sense of deference and passively appeal to a higher power that may or may not answer our calls, cries, and prayers. This process is how many of us have been taught to use these intentional rituals. We are guided to give all of our personal power over to the Minister, Preacher, or Imam. We are taught that they are the intercessor on our behalf, based on either education and/or a divine calling they have received. We place our faith, trust, and power in their hands, and follow with full confidence. The dangers in this are self-evident, and go beyond the scope of this book; suffice it to say, it is the very reason why potentially brilliant and thoughtful people are easily converted into submissive and subservient "sheeple."

In this version of ritual (where we passively participate), we have periodic and perhaps sporadic glimpses of spirit. We have "miracles" that occur when our prayers are "answered." We acknowledge the "miracle" when someone is saved from harm and death in ways that our rational minds cannot comprehend or explain. We faithfully give tribute money to our houses of worship, in order to secure our favor in the afterlife. We trust our religious leaders to be worthy of our unquestioning obedience to their selective preaching, partial teaching, and even community leeching; accepting their flaws to be normal and within the circumference of human frailty.

I like to look at this form of ritual as being more artistic than scientific. It has the forms, sounds, smells, gestures, and feeling of a deeply spiritual process, but is, by any measure, almost completely devoid of intentionally and scientifically directed spiritual power, on the part of the participants. This is what separates even our most powerful forms of ritual in the mainstream West, from the African-centered perspective and practices.

Before we explore the African-centered forms of ritual, let us place our Lodge practices into the three aforementioned levels of ritual. With all do respect, our Lodge ritual has been relegated mostly to the first two forms of ritual. Like the first level, we get "dressed" in regular fashion, we show up to our regularly scheduled meetings, and we play our roles depending on what station we are currently occupying. We go through the physical motions, verbalize a consistent script, deliver and receive memorized lectures and degree work, and have our annual functions, conferences, and special forums like clockwork. Many times we do all of these things, and many of us have been doing these things for decades, to the point to where it becomes automatic, with very little conscious thought required on our part. It's very similar to how we brush our teeth without thinking about it, or how we drive to and from work without thinking about the route.

Then there are those of us who experience our Lodge work as described in the second level of ritual presented above. We automatically give a degree of sanctity to being present in the Lodge. We have an innate respect for the presence of the GAO-TU[7] as evidenced by the V of SL that MUST be present for us to perform our works.

We open and close with prayer; we see and recognize the beauty in our form and the eloquence of our Grand Lecturers as they deliver the allegories and historical citations for our Craft. We see the Light awakened

---

7   GAOTU = Grand Architect of the Universe = God

in our EA at their I_____, we witness the strengthening of that same Light as they are P_____ on to the degree of a FC, and finally, we see the divinely inspired joy as the Light is "fully" revealed to our Brothers as they are R_____ as MM. The sanctity of our Craft permeates everything that we do within our Lodges. It is deeply embedded, although codified, in our allegories and symbolic expressions. From the rituals experienced by our new candidates all the way to our Funerary works, we recognize there is something deep about our practices.

Our Craft, just like all ancient institutions, is a hub designed to keep, protect, and conceal immense spiritual power. Those of us who know this, utilize our time in the Lodge with the intentions of utilizing this power. We find ourselves, to whatever degree we are capable, intending to gain "more Light" by participating in the various ceremonies and rituals. Just as I described above in the third level of ritual, we tend to be more passive than active in this pursuit. We relinquish our personal power to a higher being, separate and distant from ourselves.

  The difference between the Lodge expression of this level of ritual and that of our religious institutions is the fact that we, in the Lodge, do not ascribe to a "middle-man" who intervenes on our behalf for the sake of communicating with God (i.e., preacher, etc.). Everyone in the Lodge is on equal footing, as men, regardless of the individual socio-political stations they hold both in and outside the Lodge. While the WM conducts and leads us in instruction and business, and the Chaplain leads us in prayer, it is the duty of every man there present to work on their own behalf, and simultaneously for the benefit of their Brother, the Lodge, and the Craft as a whole. This is regardless of our individual religious affiliations.

  We too, have the sporadic experience of "miracle" and have our "unexplained" occurrences that we ascribe to divine intervention. We have there, hidden in our allegories, many examples of miraculous feats, especially the story of the resurrection of H.A., by the King of Israel. The building of a particular temple without the sound of tools and without any discarded materials is another miracle highlighted in our Craft. And even the notion that it only rained at night and when the Craftsmen were taking a break, but never when they were working on the Temple[8].

　　While we have certain advantages over many of our religious institutions, in regards to accessing our spiritual powers, we still fall short of becoming the spiritual scientists that our more ancient Ancestors of the Craft were. They functioned as spiritual chemists in the laboratory of Nature, learning and utilizing the spiritual anatomy of Man as their chemical tool, and creation itself provided the ingredients for working the formulas outlined in our legends, allegories, and V of SL. This my friends, is what separates these three levels of ritual from the African-centered understanding of the same.

　　Relatively few of us here in North

8　　The significance of these symbols will be explored in great detail in Symbolically Speaking, Volume 2.

America have been exposed to the moving energies of an African-based ritual, wherein we find people performing physical feats seemingly impossible under ordinary conditions. For example, while in Africa, I participated in a ritual with the Jolla. During this performance, the Jolla men blew on whistles and danced their signature dance while the women followed behind in procession, clapping pieces of metal together creating a powerful rhythmic melody. Individual Jolla men, women, and children, danced around demonstrating the power of their "juju"[9] by taking swords and cutting across their arms with no injury, or by taking a razor blade, shaving the bark of a tree to demonstrate its sharpness and then running the same blade across their tongues, eyelids, or other body parts without penetrating the skin. I was later told that this same spiritual science is what Toussaint L'Ouverture, Dutty Boukman, and others, used to successfully liberate Haiti from the French military. It was a spir-

---

9   Spiritual magic sometimes in the form of a talisman, etc.

itual protection that prevented metal from piercing the body,[10] allowing the Haitians to fight fearlessly against the firepower of the French.

Once, while attending an African ritual here in the United States, I observed one of the High Priests going into trance. The energy of this ritual was intentionally martial, and thus there were swords, fire, and a "fiery" drum cadence being played. This High Priest danced around an iron pot[11] for a few minutes before inverting his body into a "handstand," then slowly lowering his head into the pot, which was burning incense and herbs.

As he lowered himself, his legs arched over the rest of his body in such a way that he was seemingly off balance, yet was totally stable. He remained absolutely still in this position for a few minutes before raising himself back up and continuing to

---

10   I personally tested each of these tools...they are real.

11   Called a "Ting" in the 50th Hexagram of the I Ching

dance. In association with this same group, an elder once boasted to me about having undergone lung surgery, without anesthesia, by going into trance, and using only a machete in the hands of a powerful African healer/priest.

Masonically speaking, everything we do in the Lodge is a ritual. The way we open and close, the way we go from l to r, the way we perform our funeral rites, and most definitely the way we do our degree work. Each and every degree has a ritual very specific to the work and goals to be accomplished. In each of these degrees we have very specific symbols, colors, scripts, movements, and characters being portrayed. Every cap, every jewel, every geometric shape, every sign, password, grip, penalty and due-guard, are all symbolic representations of some underlying philosophy, truth, belief and/or purpose.

Our ritual is so dense and varied, even volumes such as *The Scottish Rite Ritual Monitor and Guide* by Brother Arturo de Hoyos, fail to scratch the surface of their inherent power. As stated in the opening pages as a quote from Albert Pike's ***Morals and Dogma:***

> We teach the truth of none of the legends we recite. They are to us but parables and allegories, involving and enveloping Masonic instruction; and vehicles of useful and interesting information. They represent the different phases of the human mind, its efforts and struggles to comprehend nature, God, the government of the Universe, the permitted existence of sorrow and evil. To teach us wisdom, and the folly of endeavoring to explain to ourselves that which we are not capable of understanding, we reproduce the speculations of the Philosophers, the Kabalists, the Mystagogues and the Gnostics. Every one being at liberty to apply our symbols and emblems as he thinks most consistent with truth and reason and with his own faith, we give them such an interpretation only as may be accepted by all... To honor the Deity, to regard all men as our Brethren, as children, equally dear to Him, of the Supreme Creator of the Uni-

verse, and to make himself useful to society and himself by his labor, are its teachings to its Initiates in all the Degrees.

Nothing of the mystical aspects of our Masonic ritual is touched upon in any plain or direct fashion. The intellectual and historical significance of the ritual is detailed and repeated across various sources, yet our modern literature seems to shy away from even the possibility of our ritual practices having any spiritual significance. The African-centered scholar in me has an issue accepting the notion that ritual, of any kind, is completely devoid of spiritual significance. Pike, in the above quote taken from de Hoyos' wonderful book, clearly eludes to several spiritual traditions from which Freemasonry has developed its lore, symbolism, and even certain practices, but it is left up to each individual Mason to delve as deeply or as superficially as they so desire.

Imagine if the rituals on the Scottish Rite "branch," as well as those on the York Rite "branch" of the "Masonic tree" were all conducted in such a way that the rituals intentionally had a spiritual and psychically transforming impact on the candidate going through them. What if at the conferring of the highest degree in Masonry, the newly raised Master Mason actually resurrected to a new state of mind and purpose? To our credit, many do actually report such a transformation, similar to what is experienced when a Muslim makes his Hajj, or when a Christian is baptized in the Jordan River; however, this is not the norm, nor is it the real expectation of many Brothers that go through the process.

Before, during, and after taking my Masonic degrees, I was familiar with and actively participating in several ancient African spiritual sciences. These initiations allowed me to experience, first-hand, the power of ritual when done according to the wisdom traditions of our ancient Ancestors. Prior to becoming a member of the Blue Lodge, I was initiated as a Kemetic Priest and had participated in a host of traditional African rituals and ceremonies. I had also been initiated by the Jolla in Gambia and the Ewe in Ghana, both of which contained their own spiritual sciences and ritual ceremonies.

The African-centered initiation that followed my becoming a member of a Masonic Lodge was with the Ifa spiritual tradition as a priest of Olokun. The culmination of these various African initiatic experiences, and their proximity to my Masonic journey, afforded me the unique opportunity of understanding and experiencing the similarities between the two, as well as a comparing and contrasting of what some believe to be a missing key to our Masonic journey as descendants of the African Lodge, currently called Prince Hall Freemasonry.

According to the African Shaman Malidoma Some', in his book *Ritual*:

> The abandonment of ritual can be devastating. From the spiritual viewpoint, ritual is inevitable and necessary if one is to live...The young ones are the future of the old ones. To allow this future to happen, the old ones must work with the Other-

world. When an elder fails to perform his work with respect to the spiritual, the future of this elder is threatened, not the present. Where ritual is absent, the young ones are restless or violent, there are no real elders, and the grown-ups are bewildered. The future is dim.

It is obvious that the consequences forewarned in the above quote are already upon us. As American Africans, our intentional and consistent use of African-based rituals has been systematically diminished. All manner of mechanisms have been deployed in order to get us to abandon our innate desire and need to perform rituals from the perspective of our Ancestry. For a while, and it still remains in certain pockets, regardless of who's religion and/or culture was being forced upon us, we found a way to link our ritual ways to the forms and processes of the alien culture. When forced into Catholicism, our Brothers and Sisters in Haiti, Dominican Republic and Puerto Rico linked the Orisha of Nigeria to the Saints of the Catholics, creating Santeria.

When the Protestant and Baptist forms of Christianity were infused into our worldview, during the seasoning phase[12] of European enslavement, our Ancestors figured out how to continue to use the natural elements, divination practices, herbal remedies, and the art and science of "juju," to maintain a level of sanity in the insane conditions of the plantation. Now that we are "free," it seems that we are further away from implementing these traditions than ever before.

The fraternity of Freemasonry is one of the oldest and largest in the world, with diasporic Africans making up a significant number (be they Prince Hall Affiliates or members of other Grand Lodges). I recall being in a remote village in The Gambia, sitting in a Brother by the name of Lamen's compound. Lamen did not speak English but he spoke four African languages and

---

12   The portion of enslavement where Africans were broken down and literally trained (in the behavioral psychology sense of the word) to become slaves in their thinking and behavior.

French. He was translating through a small child as he spoke to us about his experiences in life. The one word I was able to comprehend coming from his mouth was "mason." He told of his initiation and gestured as he described that he was the builder of the house that we currently sat in. His story helped me to understand that the way we, in the West, have separated the Operative from the Speculative, in more recent times, has actually diminished our ability to function in a truly free fashion.

This dichotomous, either/or way of thinking and reasoning is a deficiency acquired by our assimilation of the Western mentality and worldview. It forces us to draw separations where, in reality, there are none. Instead of asking "does" something relate, we would ask "how" does it relate. Instead of ascribing to one way of "knowing" we'd understand that there are several. This is the stuff that "worldview" is made of.

I leave you with this quote from an address delivered by Brother J. Harvey MacPherson, Lodge Spey, No. 527, entitled:

Antient Landmarks and Daily Advance

as found in the *Year Book of 1967*, Grand Lodge of Scotland:

...My personal belief is that the Craft, as we know it, goes far beyond the bounds of Freemasonry in its understood form... in the course of a somewhat chequered career in many parts of the world, I have encountered extraordinary instances of Craft S___ns being used over and beyond the bounds of Masonry.

In action, in Palestine, a wounded Syrian member of a Dervish sect[13] gave me the sign of G. and D., unmistakably and obviously, dropping his h___s in t. d. m___ts. I took him aside and, later, questioned him. He informed me that the S___n was one which belonged to his own particular Moslem sect. He was certainly not a Mason—but he had the S___n, and it had exactly the same meaning for him as it has for us.

---

13   For more information on this Dervish sect, see *Secret Practices of the Sufi Freemasons: The Islamic teachings at the heart of Alchemy* by Baron Rudolf von Sebottendorff.

Amongst the Pare Mountains, in East Africa[14], I watched two tribal elders greeting each other with a handshake. When one had moved on, I spoke to the other and gripped him in the same way as his companion had done. I have never seen a man more astonished. "When" he asked, "when were you accepted into our fetish?" He had never heard of a European being initiated into his order of things, and I told him that I had not heard of any of his tribe being initiated into my own order. His final question was staggering. He asked, "Bwana[15], where did you learn mshiko wa simba?[16]" Which means, quite literally, the g. of the l. This G. is the recognition sign amongst members of a tribal society who have adopted the l. as their emblem; and it is significant that the tribe concerned is not of Bantu origin but is Nilotic.

Again in East Africa, on a height

---

14   In the Kilimanjaro region of North East Tanzania.

15   Ki-Swahili word for "master."

16   This phrase is spoken in Ki-Swahili.

overlooking Lake Nyasa[17], I was given the privilege of initiation into a tribal society of the Wanyakyusa[18]. The S_____s which were imparted were given under a similar Obligation to our own, with similar, though not identical penalties attached. I feel, though, that the nature of the preparation of candidates lies outwith the obligatory secrets and it merits consideration. I myself was allowed to continue to wear a pair of light pants. The tribesmen who were initiated with me, however, were stripped of clothing. I was instructed to remove a signet ring from my finger so that I should carry nothing metallic. Together we stood on a sand 'pavement' which had been marked out in squares. We stood upright, our feet were squared, our arms were squared at shoulder and elbow, our thumbs were squared—and

---

17   Also known as Lake Malawi and Lago Niassa in Mozambique, is the southernmost African Great Lake in the East African Rift system, located between Malawi, Mozambique and Tanzania.

18   Also called Ngonde or Nkonde, this group of East Africans trace their Ancestry to a Nubian princess named Nyanseba.

our right hands rested on the most sacred object of the tribe—the skull of a former chief.

The examples are numerous, and their implications profound. Let us strive to make our Craft practical, and its wisdom sacred, as we continue to travel as Free and Accepted Masons descending from the African Lodge. May we forever honor our African Ancestry by putting our cultural ways and cultural world-view at the forefront of all that we do. May we continue to seek Light in ways that are most relevant to our lives, based on our circumstances, our needs, desires, and future goals set forth for us, by us. Our power is in our ritual; and the power in our ritual is based on the power of our worldview and how that resonates with our spirit. Go forward with pride, and practice our ways unapologetically; even in the face of scorn.

Ritual

Other Mind on the Matter Publications

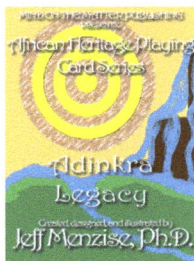

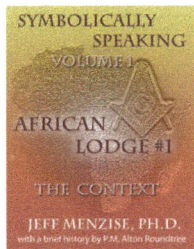

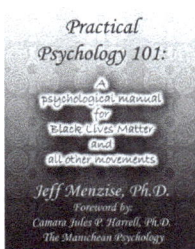

Dumbin' Down
Reflections on The Mis-Education of the Negro

JEFF MENZISE, PH.D.
FOREWORD BY RAYMOND A. WINBUSH, PH.D.

J. A. Rogers' RAMBLING RUMINATIONS
RARE WRITINGS FROM THE COLLECTION OF JOEL AUGUSTUS ROGERS

COMPILED AND EDITED BY
JEFF MENZISE, PH.D.
FOREWORD BY
MOLEFI K. ASANTE, PH.D.

MIND ON THE MATTER PUBLISHING presents...
African Heritage Playing Card Series
Adinkra Legacy
Created, designed and illustrated by
Jeff Menzise, Ph.D.

MIND ON THE MATTER PUBLISHING presents...
African Heritage Playing Card Series
VODOUN VEVE
Created, designed and illustrated by
Jeff Menzise, Ph.D.

SYMBOLICALLY SPEAKING
VOLUME 1
AFRICAN LODGE #1
THE CONTEXT
JEFF MENZISE, PH.D.
with a brief history by P.M. Alton Roundtree

Practical Psychology 101:
A psychological manual for Black Lives Matter and all other movements
Jeff Menzise, Ph.D.
Foreword by:
Camara Jules P. Harrell, Ph.D.
The Manichean Psychology

www.ingramcontent.com/pod-product-compliance
Lightning Source LLC
Chambersburg PA
CBHW050844270326
41930CB00020B/3470